Exotic Kuwaiti Recipes

Your Cookbook of Marvelous Middle-Eastern Dish Ideas!

BY: Allie Allen

COOK & ENJOY

Copyright 2021 Allie Allen

Copyright Notes

Table of Contents

Introduction

What types of food would you find in Kuwait?

They have a wide variety of dishes you'll find interesting and delicious!

Can you make Kuwaiti recipes at home?

Yes, indeed! There are many that your family will love!

When you first thought of Kuwaiti cuisine, you probably pictured falafel and hummus dishes, and those are sometimes served in the Middle Eastern country. But they also have their own unique dishes prepared in the methods they developed.

Kuwait has a desert and sub-tropical climate, yet their typical dishes include heavy soups and rice-based meals. Seafood is also important since the country is located on the Persian Gulf.

Among Kuwait's favorite food is Harees, a thick dish, like soup, made with meat and wheat that are mashed together and topped with spices.

Muttabaq Samak is another similar variation of the dishes found in neighboring Arab states. It's made with fish and rice, and the taste is divine. Read on, and learn all about the exotic dishes of Kuwait you can prepare at home…

Kuwaiti Breakfast Recipes...

Menemen – Turkish-Style Egg Breakfast

This breakfast recipe is traditionally from Turkey but is served in restaurants and homes in Kuwait and other countries. It's easy to make and extra tasty when you serve it with crusty bread.

Makes: 3-4 Servings

Cooking + Prep Time: 20 minutes

Ingredients:

- 1 tbsp. of oil, olive
- 1 finely diced, small onion, white
- 1 diced, large bell pepper, green
- 1 x 15-oz. can of tomatoes, diced, with juice
- 1 tbsp. of butter, unsalted
- Salt, sea, as needed
- Pepper, cracked, as needed
- 3 or 4 eggs, large
- Optional, for garnishing: chopped parsley or sliced chives; sliced avocado; crumbled feta cheese

Instructions:

1. Heat the oil in a large pan on med-high. Add the pepper and onion. Stir occasionally while sautéing for 5 minutes till softened.

2. Reduce heat level to med. Add the butter, tomatoes, sea salt & cracked pepper. Stir till combined evenly. Sauté for 2 minutes more till the onion is fully heated.

3. Crack the eggs atop the tomato mixture and let them cook for a minute or so. Break the yolks and stir the eggs briefly and partially into the tomatoes. Continue to cook till the eggs have reached the doneness level you desire. Serve promptly with chosen garnishes.

Sweet Vermicelli Breakfast

This is a sweet and tasty breakfast dish made often during Ramadan in Kuwait and other Arabian Gulf countries. You can add onions and eggs if you like.

Makes: 4 Servings

Cooking + Prep Time: 45 minutes

Ingredients:

- 1 lb. of vermicelli, rice
- 1 cup of sugar, granulated
- 2 to 3 tsp. of cardamom, ground
- 3 tbsp. of water, rose, if available
- 2 tbsp. of butter or oil, olive
- A pinch of saffron
- 3 quarts of water, filtered

Instructions:

1. Set the oven to broil. Place the vermicelli on trays under the broiler till it is golden brown in color. Turn if needed.

2. Remove the vermicelli from the oven. Cook in the boiling water for exactly 3 minutes. Drain it and set it aside.

3. In a large-sized pan, mix the butter or oil with the saffron, cardamom, sugar & rose water while stirring on med. heat.

4. Add the vermicelli and stir to combine. Allow to cook on the lowest heat setting for 30 minutes. Serve while warm.

Kuwaiti-Style Shakshuka

Shakshuka came originally from Northern Africa, but it is popular in many Middle Eastern countries, including Kuwait. It varies in preparation from one country to another.

Makes: 6 Servings

Cooking + Prep Time: 45 minutes

Ingredients:

- To fry: oil, olive
- 1 chopped large onion, yellow
- 2 chopped peppers, green
- 2 peeled and chopped garlic cloves
- 1 tsp. of coriander, ground
- 1 tsp. of paprika, sweet
- 1/2 tsp. of cumin, ground
- Salt, sea, as desired
- Pepper, black, as desired
- 6 chopped tomatoes, vine-ripened
- 1/2 cup of tomato sauce, no salt added
- 6 eggs, large
- 1/4 cup of chopped parsley leaves, fresh
- 1/4 cup of chopped mint leaves, fresh
- Challah or crusty bread for serving

Instructions:

1. Heat 3 tbsp. of oil in a large cast-iron skillet. Add the garlic, peppers, onion and spices. Add sea salt & black pepper. Stir occasionally while cooking for 4-6 minutes till the vegetables are softened.

2. And the tomatoes & tomato sauce and cover the skillet. Allow the mixture to simmer for 15 minutes or so. Cover. Cook a little longer, allowing the tomato mixture to thicken and reduce. Season as desired.

3. Make six wells or indentations in the tomato mixture. Crack the eggs gently into the wells. Reduce heat. Cover the skillet & cook over low heat till the egg whites have set.

4. Uncover the skillet. Add the mint and parsley. Season as desired. Serve while warm, along with challah or crusty bread.

Kuwaiti Recipes for Lunch, Dinner, Side Dishes and Appetizers…

Machboos Laham – Kuwait's National Dish

The national dish of Kuwait, this recipe includes meat, rice and stuffing, consisting of onions, split beans and raisins. It takes a while to prepare, but it's worth it for the authentic flavor.

Makes: 6 Servings

Cooking + Prep Time: 2 hours & 10 minutes

Ingredients:

For the meat portion

- 2 & 1/4 lb. of lamb (you can use chicken if you prefer)
- 2 & 1/2 quarts of water, filtered, plus more
- 1 onion, small
- 1 cinnamon stick
- 1 tsp. of peppercorns, black
- 1/2 tsp. of cloves
- 2 bay leaves, medium
- 5 cardamom pieces
- 1 tbsp. of salt, sea
- 1/4 tsp. of cinnamon, ground
- 1/4 tsp. of turmeric, ground
- A pinch of ginger, ground
- 1/4 tsp. of cumin, ground
- Salt, sea, as desired
- Pepper, black, as desired
- 1/4 tsp. threads of saffron
- 2 tbsp. of lemon juice, fresh
- 1 tbsp. of oil, olive

For rice portion

- 2 & 1/4 lb. of basmati rice
- 2 onions, medium
- 2 & 1/2 oz. of split peas, yellow
- 2 & 1/2 oz. of raisins, dark
- 1 tbsp. of oil, olive
- A pinch of cinnamon, ground
- Salt, sea as desired
- 1/2 tsp. of sugar, granulated
- Cloves, ground, as desired
- Pepper, black, as desired

Instructions:

1. Remove the raisins from the packaging and soak in water while you're preparing the other ingredients. Drain when ready to use them.

2. Preheat the oven to 395F.

3. Cut the lamb in cubes. In a large-sized pot, combine the lamb cubes with the water, whole spices, 1 quartered, small onion and sea salt.

4. Bring the mixture to a boil. Once the water is boiling, remove the froth on top. Cover the pot. Allow the mixture to cook for 1 1/2 hours on med-low heat.

5. To prepare the "stuffing" (which actually isn't "stuffed" into anything – it's just what they call it), cover the split peas in a small pan with filtered water. Add sea salt. Bring to a boil on med-high heat. Cover the pan. Reduce heat level to med-low. Cook till the peas become tender, 18-20 minutes. Drain. Set the mixture aside.

6. Chop the onions. Sauté in the olive oil till golden brown and tender.

7. Reduce heat level to med-low. Add the split peas & raisins. Add the cloves, cinnamon, sea salt, granulated sugar & ground pepper. Continue cooking till all of the ingredients are well combined, several minutes or so. Remove from heat. Set the mixture aside.

8. After 80-90 minutes, drain the lamb cubes in a colander over a large-sized bowl. Save the stock. Discard the whole spices.

9. Mix the ground spices. Then, rub the dry ingredients over the lamb cubes. Arrange them on a baking pan.

10. Mix the saffron and water with the lemon juice, oil & 1 tbsp. the lamb stock. Drizzle the mixture over the lamb. Cover a baking pan with foil. Place in the 395F oven for 12-15 minutes.

11. Wash & drain the rice a few times till the water is running clear. Cover with filtered water. Add sea salt & mix.

12. Drain the water from the rice. In a medium pan, add the rice and lamb stock so that the rice is covered by 1 inch or so. Bring the mixture to a boil on high heat, then cover the pan and reduce heat level to med-low. Cook for 15 to 20 minutes till the rice has absorbed the liquid and is fluffy and cooked.

13. Fold the lamb and "stuffing." Serve atop the rice. Drizzle with the remainder of saffron water and serve.

Jareesh

This is a popular, traditional dish in countries in the Arabian Peninsula, including Kuwait. It's made with crushed wheat and chicken cooked along with milk, and it has a unique taste.

Makes: 3-5 Servings

Cooking + Prep Time: 1 hour & 55 minutes + 2 hours resting time

Ingredients:

- 1 tomato, sliced
- 3 & 1/2 oz. of onions, medium
- 3 & 1/3 tbsp. of oil, corn
- 1 & 3/4 oz. of garlic-ginger paste
- 1 lb. of thighs, chicken
- 1 & 3/4 oz. of tomato paste, no salt added
- 1/2 tbsp. of powdered cumin
- 1/2 tbsp. of powdered turmeric
- 1/2 tbsp. of powdered coriander
- 1/2 tbsp. of pepper, white, ground
- 2 lemons, fresh
- 3 cloves, fresh
- 2 bay leaves, medium
- Water, filtered, as needed
- Salt, kosher, as desired
- 8 & 3/4 oz. of wheat, broken
- 1 & 3/4 oz. of yogurt, plain
- Oil, corn, as needed
- Onions, white, as needed
- Green chilies, fresh, for garnishing

Instructions:

1. Slice the tomato and onions finely.

2. Heat the oil in a deep large pot. Add the garlic-ginger paste. Sauté till the no raw smell remains, 2 to 3 minutes.

3. Add the chicken. Fry on each side for 10 to 15 minutes, till the chicken is golden in color.

4. Add the onions, tomato and tomato paste to the chicken. Sauté thoroughly. Add the powdered cumin, turmeric, coriander and white pepper. Combine well.

5. Add water to the pot. Prick the lemon with a knife. Add to the pot. Add the sea salt, cloves and bay leaves. Cover. Cook till the chicken has cooked halfway.

6. Remove the pieces of chicken from the gravy. Place on a cookie sheet.

7. Heat the oven to 350F. Roast the chicken in the oven till it has turned golden brown, 10 minutes or so.

8. Add the broken wheat to the chicken stock. Add more water if needed. Cover the pot. Cook till the wheat is done cooking, 10 to 15 minutes.

9. Add the yogurt to the wheat mixture and gently stir. You want the consistency that is creamy.

10. Heat corn oil in a pot. Add the onions and fry till they are dark golden. Using the same oil, fry green chilies lightly.

11. Place Jareesh on serving plates. Top with the chicken, caramelized onions & garnish with the green chilies. Serve.

Kuwaiti Falafel

This simple falafel recipe uses chickpeas and assorted seasonings, creating a dish with a crispy outside and moist and fluffy inside. It's sold on the street corners in many Middle Eastern countries.

Makes: 2 Servings

Cooking + Prep Time: 20 minutes

Ingredients:

- 1 x 15-oz. can of drained, rinsed chickpeas
- 1 tbsp. of garlic, minced
- 1 finely chopped onion, medium
- 2 tbsp. of fresh parsley, chopped finely
- 1 tsp. of coriander, ground
- 3/4 tsp. of cumin, ground
- 1/2 tsp. of salt, kosher
- Pepper, black, as desired
- 2 tbsp. of flour, all-purpose
- To fry: 3 cups of oil, vegetable

Instructions:

1. Combine the chickpeas with the onion, garlic, coriander, parsley, salt, cumin & pepper, as desired, in medium-sized bowl. Add the flour. Mix well.

2. Mash the chickpeas, mixing all of the ingredients together well. You should have a thick paste.

3. Form the mixture in ping-pong-sized balls. Flatten a bit.

4. Fry in 2" of the 350F oil for 2-5 minutes, till golden brown. Remove from the pan. Drain on a plate lined with paper towels and serve.

Mandi Laham – Lamb Mandi

This traditional meal was originally served in Yemen. It is now popular in many Arab countries, including Kuwait. The lamb pairs well with rice and the recipe's spice mixture.

Makes: 5 Servings

Cooking + Prep Time: 1 hour & 20 minutes + 3-4 hours marinating time

Ingredients:

- 2 & 1/4 lb. of mutton
- 2 cups of rice, soaked
- 2 carrots, grated
- 2 chili peppers, sliced
- 3 tbsp. of oil, olive
- 1/2 cup of almonds
- 4 cups of chicken stock, low sodium
- Salt, kosher, as needed
- 4 cardamoms, green
- 4 cloves, fresh
- Pepper, black, as needed
- A pinch of nutmeg, ground
- 2 bay leaves, medium
- 1 tsp. of powdered ginger
- 4 sliced lemons, fresh
- 1 cup of water, filtered

Instructions:

1. To a grinder, add the cloves, cardamoms, bay leaves, nutmeg, ginger and pepper. Grind thoroughly.

2. Place the spices in a medium bowl. Add 2 tbsp. of the oil, the lemon slices, filtered water and kosher salt as needed.

3. Apply the spice mixture to the mutton. Allow to marinate for 3-4 hours.

4. Pack the mutton with foil in a pan. Bake in the 350F oven for 35-40 minutes.

5. Cook till the water has dried and remove the pan from the oven.

6. Heat the remainder of oil in a medium pan. Add the chicken stock. Boil for 15-20 minutes. Add 1 tsp. of the spice mixture.

7. Add the rice and salt. Cook till only a bit of the water remains. Mix the carrots and peppers.

8. Cover the mixture tightly. Steam for 10 to 15 minutes over low heat.

9. When the rice is done, place it on a platter. Add the mutton. Use the almonds to garnish, then serve while hot.

Chicken & Rice Biryani

As is the case with many dishes in the Middle East, each of the countries has variations. The main ingredients here are chicken, saffron, berries and rice, and they are generally included in most countries.

Makes: 4 Servings

Cooking + Prep Time: 1 hour & 20 minutes

Ingredients:

For saffron infusion

- 3 tbsp. of very hot water, filtered
- 20 crushed saffron threads
- For chicken
- 2 chicken breasts & 2 chicken thighs
- 1 tbsp. of oil, olive
- Salt, kosher & pepper, black, as desired

For sauce

- 1 tbsp. of oil, olive
- 1 peeled, diced onion, medium
- 2 peeled, minced garlic cloves
- 3 tbsp. of tomato paste, no salt added
- 1 & 1/2 cups of water, filtered
- 1/2 tsp. of salt, kosher, +/- as desired
- 1/2 tsp. of pepper, black, +/- as desired
- 1/2 tsp. of turmeric, ground

For rice

- 2 & 3/4 cups of water, filtered
- 1 cup of rice, Basmati
- 1 tbsp. of saffron-infused water
- Salt, kosher, as desired
- 1/2 cup of cranberries, dried

Instructions:

1. To bloom the saffron, crush the threads using your fingers. Add to a small-sized bowl. Add the heated water. Then, allow it to sit for about 15 minutes.

2. To prepare the chicken, heat the oil in a skillet. Add the chicken with the skin side facing down. Season as desired. Cook till both of the sides have lightly browned, 8-10 minutes. Remove the chicken from the skillet. Set it aside.

3. Add the oil to a skillet. Add the onion. Sauté till the onion has become translucent. Add the garlic and stir. Continue to cook for several seconds more.

4. Stir in the tomato paste. Add 2 tbsp. of the saffron water, the water and turmeric. Season as desired.

5. Add the chicken back to the skillet. Cover. Lower heat to med-low. Cook till the chicken becomes tender and is cooked fully through 30-40 minutes.

6. To make the saffron rice, add the water and rice to a pot. Bring to boil. Cover the pot. Reduce heat level to low. Cook for 12-15 minutes till the rice absorbs all of the water. Remove the pot from heat. Season as desired. Add the last saffron water. Add the cranberries and stir. Serve the chicken with the sauce over the rice.

Middle Eastern Chorba

Chorba is a multi-flavored soup with tomatoes, chickpeas & spices. It's a popular Middle Eastern soup, especially during Ramadan.

Makes: 4-6 Servings

Cooking + Prep Time: 1 hour & 10 minutes + overnight soaking time for chickpeas

Ingredients:

- 1 lb. of stew meat, beef or loin chops, lamb
- 10 cups of water
- 2 finely minced onions, medium
- 3 peeled, de-seeded and crushed tomatoes, ripe
- 3 thinly sliced carrots, medium
- 2 thinly sliced stalks of celery
- 3 chopped potatoes, medium
- 2 chopped turnips, small
- 1/4 cup of finely chopped parsley, fresh
- 2 tbsp. of tomato paste – no salt added
- 1 tsp. of pepper, black
- 1 tsp. of salt, kosher
- 1/4 cup of lemon juice, fresh
- 1/4 tsp. of turmeric, ground
- 1/4 tsp. of saffron
- 1/4 tsp. of ginger, ground
- 1 & 1/2 cups of garbanzos or chickpeas, dried – soak them overnight

Instructions:

1. Place the meat & vegetables (with the exception of the tomatoes) in a large pan. Add the water. Bring to boil.

2. Add the tomatoes & tomato paste and stir gently.

3. Add the lemon juice, chickpeas and spices and stir slowly.

4. Reduce heat level to low. Allow the soup to simmer covered till the chickpeas and meat are done, 30-35 minutes. Serve.

Tahini Noodles

In this tahini-sauce and pasta dish, the soy sauce adds a bit of saltiness, and the honey balances the lemon's acid. The red pepper, ginger and garlic add heat.

Makes: 4 Servings

Cooking + Prep Time: 1/2 hour

Ingredients:

- 1/2 lb. of fettuccine
- 1/2 cup of sesame paste
- 1/2 cup of water, filtered
- 1 tbsp. of soy sauce, low sodium
- 1 tbsp. of lemon juice, fresh
- 1 tsp. of honey, pure
- 1 tsp. of ginger, freshly grated
- 1 peeled, grated garlic clove
- A pinch of crushed pepper flakes, red, +/- as desired

For garnishing: sesame seeds, sliced scallions

Instructions:

1. Cook the pasta using the instructions on the package.

2. In a medium bowl, whisk together the water, sesame paste, lemon juice, soy sauce, ginger, honey, pepper flakes and garlic till smooth.

3. Drain the cooked pasta. Toss with the tahini sauce. Top with scallions & sesame seeds and serve.

Fried Fish & Rice – Mutabbaq Samak

This recipe actually looks more difficult in print than it is. Among various Arab seafood recipes, it is a simple way to prepare the fish.

Makes: 2 Servings

Cooking + Prep Time: 1 & 1/2 hours + 1 hour marinating time

Ingredients:

- 2 silver pomfret fishes (zubaidi fish), gutted – you can use any whitefish
- Sea salt, as desired
- Pepper, black, as desired
- 1 & 3/4 tsp. Middle Eastern spice blend (Baharat), prepared
- 1/4 tsp. of turmeric, ground
- 4 tbsp. of lemon juice, fresh
- 2 minced garlic cloves, large
- 3/4 cup of basmati rice, white
- Water, filtered, as needed
- 1 cinnamon stick
- 2 bruised cardamom pods, fresh
- 1 clove, fresh (not a garlic clove)
- 2 limes, dried, pierced
- 3 tbsp. of oil, olive
- 2 cooking onions, small
- Lime & lemon wedges, fresh, for serving

Instructions:

1. Wash the fish and leave the heads intact. Remove the scales and gut the fish.

2. Wash the rice thoroughly. Allow to soak for 20 to 30 minutes.

3. Bring a large pot of water to boil. Add the fish, clove, cinnamon stick and cardamom pods. Simmer till cooked well.

4. Remove the fish from the pot. Reserve the cooking water.

5. Cut slashes across the fish. Rub on the spice mixture & minced garlic. Pour some lemon juice (fresh) over the fish. Place in the refrigerator for 1 to 1 & 1/2 hours.

6. Use the fish cooking water to cook the rice. Add the dried lime and sea salt as needed.

7. Heat the oil in a pan. Fry the onions till golden and soft while adding the turmeric, sea salt as desired and 1/4 tsp. of the Middle Eastern spice mixture (Baharat).

8. Mix 2/3 of the onions in the cooked rice. Sprinkle the remainder of onions on the top.

9. After the fish is done marinating, pat it dry using paper towels.

10. Preheat the oven to 275 degrees F.

11. Heat 1/2 inch of olive oil till hot in a medium pan. Fry the fish one then another, till both are golden brown in color. Drain them on a plate lined with paper towels.

12. Place the dish atop the rice and cover it with foil. Place in the 275F oven for 1 hour. Serve with lime & lemon wedges.

Harira Lentil Soup

This is a classic soup made with tomatoes, chickpeas, lentils, meat, spices and herbs. It's a satisfying and filling dish.

Makes: 6-8 Servings

Cooking + Prep Time: 2 & 1/2 hours + 8 hours chickpea & lentil soaking time

Ingredients:

- 3 tbsp. of oil, vegetable
- 1/2 lb. of 1/2"-cubed lamb, chicken or beef
- 6 peeled, de-seeded, pureed tomatoes, large
- 1 tbsp. of salt, kosher
- 1/2 tsp. of turmeric, ground
- 1/4 cup of finely chopped parsley leaves
- 1/4 cup of finely chopped cilantro leaves
- 1 finely chopped celery stalk, leaves included
- 1 & 1/2 tsp. of pepper, ground
- 1 tsp. of cinnamon, ground
- 1 tbsp. of ginger, ground
- 1 grated onion, large
- 1 handful of chickpeas, dried – soak them overnight and peel
- 11 cups of water, filtered
- 3 tbsp. of lentils, dried – soak overnight
- 3 tbsp. of tomato paste, no salt added – mix in 1 cup of water, filtered
- 2 tbsp. of rice, uncooked
- To thicken soup
- 1 cup of flour, all-purpose
- 2 cups of water, filtered

To garnish: parsley, chopped

Instructions:

1. Heat the oil in the large pressure cooker. Add the meat.

2. Cook for several minutes and stir, browning all sides.

3. To prepare the stock, add the tomatoes, turmeric, salt, cilantro, parsley, ground pepper, celery, ginger, cinnamon, chickpeas and onion. Stir. Add 3 cups of the water.

4. Cover the pressure cooker tightly. Heat on high till you achieve pressure. Reduce heat level to med. Cook for 20-30 minutes. Then, remove from heat. Release pressure.

5. To prepare the soup, add the tomato paste mixture, lentils and last 8 cups of the water. Keep the rice close by, but do not add it just yet.

6. Cover the pot. Heat the soup on high till you achieve pressure. Reduce heat level to medium. Continue to cook.

7. Cook the soup for 1/2 hour on pressure. Release pressure. Add the rice. Cover. Cook for 15 more minutes on pressure. Taste and adjust seasoning.

8. To thicken the soup as it cooks, mix the water and flour together. Combine well.

9. To finish the soup, bring the soup to a full simmer. In a slow and thin stream, add 1/2 of the flour mixture. Constantly stir and keep the soup at simmer.

10. Add 1/2 more of the flour mixture. The soup will start thickening. The thickness is your choice.

11. Simmer thickened the soup and occasionally stir for 5-10 minutes to cook away flour taste. Remove the soup from heat. Garnish with parsley and serve.

Tashreeb

The word "tashreeb" refers to Arab dishes that feature bread soaked with broth, then topped with vegetables or meat. It has many variations, and it is a flavorful and filling meal.

Makes: Various # of Servings

Cooking + Prep Time: 1 & 1/2 hour

Ingredients:

For the lamb

- 2 & 1/4 lb. of lamb on bone
- 2 tbsp. of oil, olive
- 5 cardamom pods
- 1 halved cinnamon stick
- 1 piece of crushed mastic or 1/2 tsp. of vanilla, pure
- 1/2 sliced onion, medium
- Water

For the sauce

- 2 tbsp. of butter, unsalted
- 2 half-moon-sliced onions, medium
- 2 chopped tomatoes, large
- 1 can of chickpeas, drained
- 2 pieces of pierced dry limes (loomi)
- 1 & 1/2 tbsp. of Middle Eastern spice blend
- 1 tbsp. of powdered curry
- 2 tbsp. of tomato paste, no salt added
- Salt, kosher & pepper, ground, as desired
- Flatbread for serving

Instructions:

1. In a large-sized pot, brown the lamb in the oil. Add the onion, spices & mastic or vanilla. Add sufficient water that the lamb is covered by 3 inches. Cook the lamb till tender.

2. Drain and cube the lamb. Reserve the stock. Set them aside.

3. In the same pot, add the butter and use to sauté the onions. Add salt so that the onions will soften and not caramelize.

4. Once the onions are soft, add the chickpeas, tomatoes, spice blend, dried lime and powdered curry. Sauté for several minutes. Add the tomato paste. Be sure to mix all of the ingredients well. Cook for several minutes, then add the stock.

5. Bring the mixture to boil, then lower heat. Cook for 30 to 40 minutes till the tomatoes and onions have softened fully and the stew has thickened slightly.

6. Tear bread onto each individual serving plate. Top with the stew. Serve.

Doner Kebabs

If you've had Greek gyros before, you are already familiar with the wonderful taste of doner kebabs. They are usually made with lamb, beef or both.

Makes: 4 Servings

Cooking + Prep Time: 2 hours & 25 minutes

Ingredients:

For kebab

- 1 lb. of lamb, ground or 1/2 lb. each of ground beef & ground lamb
- 1 egg, large
- 4 peeled, minced garlic cloves
- 1 tsp. of cumin, ground
- 1 tsp. of coriander, ground
- 1 tsp. of paprika, smoked
- 1 tsp. of oregano, dried
- 1/2 tsp. of salt, kosher
- 1/4 tsp. of pepper, black
- 1 tbsp. of oil, olive + extra for pan

For sandwich

- 4 flatbreads, pita or naan, large
- 1 cup of lettuce leaves, assorted
- 1 sliced tomato, large
- 1/2 sliced cucumber, medium
- 1/4 peeled, sliced large onion, red
- Tahini sauce

Instructions:

1. Preheat the oven to 350F.

2. In a large-sized bowl, combine the meat, garlic, egg, coriander, cumin, oregano, paprika, kosher salt & ground pepper.

3. Place the mixture in a greased 9" x 5" loaf pan. Cook in the 350F oven till the top is golden brown, about 1/2 hour.

4. Cool fully and wrap in foil. Refrigerate till firm.

5. To reheat the kebab, add the oil to a large-sized skillet. Slice the loaf thinly. Crisp the slices in the hot pan for several minutes.

6. Assemble the sandwiches with the pita, naan or flatbread, warmed & toasted. Spread the kebab and some tahini sauce on. Add the lettuce, cucumbers, tomatoes and onions. Top with the additional sauce and serve.

Kuwaiti Kibda – Fried Liver

This is a popular Arab Gulf dish, and it's trending as a popular meal in many other regions. It's simple to make and tastes delicious.

Makes: 2 Servings

Cooking + Prep Time: 15 minutes

Ingredients:

- 1 lb. of liver, beef
- 1/2 cup of sliced peppers, green
- 1 tsp. of grated garlic, fresh
- 1 tsp. of lemon juice, fresh
- 1 tbsp. of margarine, light
- 2 tbsp. of oil, olive
- Pepper, black, as desired
- Sauce, hot, as desired
- Salt, kosher, as desired
- Crusty bread for serving

Instructions:

1. Wash the liver. Slice and add the garlic and green peppers. Combine well.

2. Heat the margarine and oil in a medium pan. Add the liver mixture and season with salt & hot sauce, as desired. Cook till the liver is fully done.

3. Turn heat off. Mix the lemon juice into the pan. Serve the mixture warm with crusty bread.

Kuwaiti Murabyan – Spiced Shrimp with Rice

This is a rice pilaf and shrimp dish that is wonderfully fragrant with herbs and spices. The version includes plenty of butter and a sweet yet savory flavor from sautéed onions.

Makes: 4 Servings

Cooking + Prep Time: 55 minutes

Ingredients:

- 1/2 tbsp. of oil, olive
- 1/2 lengthwise-sliced onion, large

For spice mixture

- 1/4 tsp. of pepper, ground
- 1 garlic clove – mash with:
- 1/2 tbsp. grated ginger, fresh
- 1 tsp. of coriander, fresh
- 1 lb. of peeled & deveined shrimp, large or medium
- 1 large tomato, thick-sliced
- 2 tsp. of salt, sea
- 2 cups of water, filtered
- 2 cups of rice, basmati

For topping

- 1/8 cup of oil, olive
- 1 lengthwise-sliced onion, yellow
- 1/4 tsp. of cardamom, ground
- 1/4 tsp. of pepper, ground
- 1/2 tsp. of powdered curry
- 1/2 tsp. of turmeric, ground
- 1/4 tsp. of cloves, ground
- 1/4 tsp. of black, dried lime, grated (called "loomi" in Arab countries)
- 1/4 cup of chopped cilantro, fresh
- 1 garlic clove, fresh – mash with:
- 1/2 tsp. of coriander, fresh
- 1/4 tsp. of pepper, black
- 1 pound of peeled, deveined shrimp, medium or large

Instructions:

1. Heat the oil in a pan on med. heat.

2. Add the onion. Sauté till golden brown in color. Add the garlic, pepper and spice mixture.

3. Add 1 lb. of the shrimp with the tomato. Cook on med. heat for 10-12 minutes.

4. Add the water & kosher salt. Bring to boil.

5. Add the rice. Stir, mixing all of the ingredients together well.

6. Reduce the heat to med-low. Simmer till rice absorbs water. Remove from heat. Set aside.

7. To prepare the topping, sauté the onion in the oil till golden brown in color. Add the spices, garlic mash mixture, grated lime and cilantro. Stir well.

8. Add the shrimp. Sauté till it is cooked through well.

9. Add the rice mixture to a platter. Add the shrimp mixture and spoon it over the top. Serve.

Kuwaiti-Style Vegetable Stew

Vegetable stew has many incarnations all over the world. In this recipe, the Kuwaiti version has many vegetables you have probably already had at home, as well as tomato paste & coriander.

Makes: 3 Servings

Cooking + Prep Time: 35 minutes

Ingredients:

- 1 carrot, large
- 1 potato, large
- 2 marrow gourds or squashes
- 2 tbsp. of oil, olive
- 1 1" piece of chopped ginger, fresh
- 1 minced onion, medium
- 1/2 tsp. of powdered turmeric
- 1 tsp. of powdered cumin
- 1 minced tomato, large
- 1/2 tsp. of chili powder
- 4 & 1/2 oz. of tomato paste, no salt added
- 2 cups of water
- 2 vegetable stock cubes
- Salt, kosher, as desired
- Pepper, ground, as desired

To garnish: coriander leaves, fresh

Instructions:

1. Peel the vegetables. Chop into sticks.

2. Heat the oil in a medium pot. Fry the ginger for 2-3 minutes. Add the onion. Sauté till it softens.

3. Add the powders. Sauté for 1 minute or so. Add the tomato paste and tomato. Cook till the oil has floated to the top.

4. Add the vegetables, water and vegetable stock cubes.

5. Keep the pot over high heat till the mixture boils. Reduce heat and simmer till the veggies are cooked.

6. Season as desired. Garnish with coriander leaves and serve while warm.

Middle Eastern Ful Medammes

If you like hummus, this dish should be a favorite for you. It's a dip made from fava beans, often eaten with warmed pita bread.

Makes: 6 Servings

Cooking + Prep Time: 20 minutes

Ingredients:

- 1 x 15-oz. can of beans, fava
- 1 tsp. of garlic, minced
- 1/2 tsp. of lemon juice, freshly squeezed
- 1 tbsp. of tahini sauce
- A pinch of salt, kosher
- 3 tbsp. of water, hot
- 1 tbsp. of oil, olive
- Optional, for garnishing: finely chopped parsley, fresh
- Pita bread, heated, for serving

Instructions:

1. In a medium pot, combine the fava beans and their liquid with the garlic and lemon juice. Bring to boil. Remove the pot from heat.

2. Drain excess liquid. Mash the fava beans coarsely using a potato masher or fork in the pot. Return the pot to low heat. Add the salt and tahini and heated water, then the oil, after another. Stir till the consistency is as you desire. Use parsley to garnish if desired. Serve with heated pita bread.

Maqlooba – Upside-Down Cooked Rice

This is a simple dish to prepare, originally made in Palestine. It tastes best when served with yogurt alongside.

Makes: 8 Servings

Cooking + Prep Time: 1 & 1/2 hour

Ingredients:

- 2 & 1/2 cups of rice, Basmati
- 2 tbsp. of oil, olive
- 1 chopped onion, large
- 1 lb. of lamb or beef, minced
- 1 tsp. of salt, kosher
- 1 tsp. of allspice
- Pepper, coarsely crushed, as desired
- 3 cups of chicken stock, low sodium
- 1 bite size cubed cauliflower, small – grilled or roasted
- 1 quartered, cubed eggplant, large
- 1 quartered, cubed zucchini
- 1 cubed bell pepper, red
- 2 ring-sliced tomatoes, ripe

For serving

- 1 handful of chopped parsley, fresh
- 1 oz. of pine nuts
- Yogurt, plain – serve on the side

Instructions:

1. Rinse, then drain the rice. Set it aside.

2. Heat the oil in a pan on med. heat.

3. Sauté the onions in the pan for 3 to 4 minutes.

4. Add the meat, allspice, kosher salt and pepper to the pan. Stir well. Brown the meat on all of the sides & cook for 8-10 minutes over med-high.

5. Grease a pan and add the tomatoes. Season as desired. Add the meat. Pack in and flatten an atop layer of the tomatoes. Season as desired. Add the vegetables and flatten a layer. Season as desired. Add the rice and flatten a layer. Season as desired.

6. Hold the rice down with a small-sized plate. Pour in the stock. Turn heat to high for 3 minutes till the mixture simmers.

7. Place a lid on the pan. Turn heat down. Cook for 40-45 minutes. If the rice is not yet done, cook for 5-10 minutes longer.

8. Place a large platter or plate over the pan. Turn upside down and invert the rice onto the platter. If it collapses, that's fine, but it should stay somewhat in the form of the pan.

9. Scatter with the parsley and pine nuts. Serve with yogurt.

Middle Eastern Chicken Salad

Salads make wonderful side dishes during warm weather, but they're not usually hearty enough to make a meal. Just add pita bread and grilled chicken to round this salad into a main entrée.

Makes: 4 Servings

Cooking + Prep Time: 1 & 1/2 hour + 1 hour marinating time

Ingredients:

- Lemon dressing, prepared

For salad

- 4 chicken breasts, boneless, skinless
- 2 cups of spinach, baby, or any salad green types
- 1/2 peeled, thinly sliced onion, red
- 2 cups of halved tomatoes, cherry
- 1/2 cup of pitted, halved black olives
- 1/2 cup of crumbled feta cheese
- 4 rounds of pita bread

Instructions:

1. Reserve 1/2 of the dressing in a bowl to use as a topping.

2. Add the chicken breasts in the other 1/2 of the dressing in a bowl. Coat well. Cover with cling wrap. Then, place in the refrigerator for an hour or so, and no longer than four hours.

3. Heat the grill to 400F.

4. Grill the chicken on the first side for 5 minutes and flip. Grill for 5 minutes more on the other side till it has cooked through with no pink remaining.

5. Slice the chicken meat lengthwise.

6. In a separate bowl, toss the greens together with the tomatoes, olives, feta cheese and sliced onions. Pour the dressing over the top. Toss well.

7. Assemble the salad on a platter. Top with the toasted pita bread and chicken slices. Serve.

Middle Eastern Khubz Flatbread

Khubz is a type of Middle Eastern pita or bread made with wheat flour and baked in well-heated ovens. This traditional Kuwaiti bread is a staple in their local diet.

Makes: 6 Servings

Cooking + Prep Time: 1 hour & 45 minutes + 1 hour & 30 minutes rising time

Ingredients:

- 1 & 1/2 cups of water, warm
- 1 & 1/4 oz. pkg. of dry yeast, active
- 1 & 1/2 tsp. of salt, kosher
- 3 cups of sifted flour, all-purpose plus more for dusting
- 1 tbsp. of oil, vegetable

Instructions:

1. Pour the warm water in a large-sized bowl. Add the yeast and stir till it dissolves. Add the salt.

2. Begin to gradually add the oil and flour as you knead till the dough is elastic and smooth.

3. Place the dough in a greased large bowl. Turn the dough and grease each side.

4. Cover the dough with a dry towel. Allow to rise in a warm area for 1 & 1/2 hours till it doubles in size.

5. Preheat the oven to 375F.

6. Gently punch the dough. Divide it into 12 equal balls. Shape till smooth.

7. Place the balls on a lightly floured surface. Then, lightly dust the tops using flour. Cover with a clean towel. Allow to rest for about 15 minutes.

8. Roll the balls out in circles six inches in diameter. Place them on greased cookie sheets.

9. Bake in the 375F oven for 10-12 minutes till the bread has puffed. Don't leave it unattended in the oven. Remove and serve.

Beef & Green Bean Stew

You can make this a vegetarian stew by leaving out the meat and serving on rice or flatbread like naan or pita. The tomato sauce and warm spices make it a true comfort dish, with or without the meat.

Makes: 4 Servings

Cooking + Prep Time: 2 hours & 20 minutes

Ingredients:

- 2 tbsp. of oil, olive
- 1 lb. of stew meat, cubed, beef or lamb
- 1 peeled, chopped onion, medium
- 2 peeled, minced garlic cloves
- 1 x 16-oz. can of tomatoes, crushed
- 1/2 tsp. of cumin, ground
- 1 tsp. of coriander, ground
- 1/8 tsp. of allspice, ground
- 1 tsp. of salt, kosher, as desired
- 1/2 tsp. of pepper, ground, as desired
- 8 cups of water, filtered
- 1 x 4-oz. can of tomato puree, no salt added
- 1 lb. of green beans, fresh or frozen
- White rice, cooked

Instructions:

1. Add the oil to a large-sized pot. Add the stew meat. Brown on each side.

2. Add the garlic and onion. Add tomatoes and stir the mixture well.

3. Add the allspice, coriander and cumin. Season as desired.

4. Add the water, then the tomato puree. Combine well. Add the green beans. Bring the mixture to boil. Reduce heat level to low. Simmer till the meat is done and tender, 2 hours. The sauce will thicken as it is cooking. Serve on white rice.

Chicken Shawarma

This is a wonderful pita sandwich that will fill you up like a meal. It's made using seasoned sliced chicken, along with vegetables and a sauce, in pita bread.

Makes: 4 Servings

Cooking + Prep Time: 1 hour + 8 hours marinating time

Ingredients:

- Marinade, prepared, for chicken

For chicken

- 1 & 1/2 lb. of thinly cut chicken breasts or thighs, skinless, boneless

For sauce

- 1 cup of tahini sauce
- 2 crushed garlic cloves
- 1/4 cup of lemon juice, fresh squeezed
- 2 tbsp. of yogurt, plain

For sandwich

- 1 thinly sliced onion
- 1-2 thinly sliced tomatoes, vine ripe
- 1 thinly sliced cucumber, medium
- 1/2 cup of finely chopped parsley, fresh
- 1/2 tsp. of sumac
- Optional: sliced pickles
- 4 pita breads, large

Instructions:

1. Add the chicken to a large bowl and coat with the marinade. Then, cover the bowl and place in the refrigerator for 8 hours minimum.

2. In a stock pot, cook the chicken on med. heat for 18-20 minutes till it's done. Do not overcook the meat. If it becomes a bit dry, add several tbsp. of water.

3. When the chicken is done, leave it in large slices or shred.

4. To prepare the sauce, mix the tahini, garlic, lemon juice & yogurt together in a medium bowl. Combine well and set the bowl aside.

5. In a large bowl, add the cucumber, onion and tomatoes. Sprinkle with the sumac. Add parsley and add pickle slices if using. Set the bowl aside.

6. Place the chicken pieces or shreds on the pitas till they cover 1/4 of the bread surface. Add the vegetables. Then, pour some of the sauce over the chicken and vegetables. Roll as you would do a burrito. Serve.

Asparagus & Tomato Salad

This is a Kuwaiti version of bread salad. It usually includes fried or toasted pita bread. The vegetables can be tweaked to include your favorite ones.

Makes: 2 Servings

Cooking + Prep Time: 25 minutes

Ingredients:

- 1 round of pita bread
- 1 tbsp. of oil, olive
- 1 peeled, minced garlic clove
- 1 seeded, diced tomato, ripe
- 8-10 spears of asparagus
- 1/4 tsp. of sumac
- Kosher salt, as desired
- Pepper, black, as desired
- 1 tbsp. of lemon juice, freshly squeezed

Instructions:

1. Toast the pita lightly in the oven or toaster. Cut in small pieces.

2. Add the oil and garlic to a skillet. Sauté till the garlic is slightly translucent, about 1 minute. Don't let it burn.

3. Add the tomato. Continue to cook over med-low for 1 minute more.

4. Peel the asparagus stems if thick. Thinly slice them into diagonal pieces. Add them to the pan. Continue to cook for 1 minute more.

5. Season using the sumac, kosher salt & black pepper. Stir in the pieces of pita bread. Cook for another 1-2 minutes till the pita pieces absorb flavors. Finish the dish with the lemon juice. Serve while warm.

Cheese Fatayer

Fatayer is an Arabic style bread pocket you can fill with many types of fillings. Meat, cheese and spinach are some of the most popular fillings. This recipe uses cheese.

Makes: 16 Servings

Cooking + Prep Time: 1 hour & 40 minutes

Ingredients:

- Dough, prepared, refrigerated
- Oil for brushing

For cheese filling

- 1 cup of cheese, feta
- 2 tbsp. of chopped parsley, fresh
- 2 tbsp. of mint, fresh or dried
- 1 egg, large

Instructions:

1. Preheat the oven to 400F.

2. Prepare the filling by thoroughly combining the filling ingredients together.

3. Divide the dough into halves. Roll into rectangles.

4. Spread 1/2 of the filling in each of the rectangles. Roll, forming logs.

5. Cut the logs in 1-2" lengths. Brush with oil.

6. Make indentations in the middle of the logs.

7. Bake in the 400F oven for 12-15 minutes. Allow to cool and serve.

Tahini Baked White Fish

This delicious yet simple recipe of fish and tahini is a favorite in Kuwait. Select a white fish like halibut, snapper or tilapia.

Makes: 4 Servings

Cooking + Prep Time: 20 minutes

Ingredients:

- 1 thinly sliced onion, medium
- 4 x 4-5 oz. fillets, white fish
- 1 tsp. of thyme leaves, fresh
- Salt, kosher, as desired
- Pepper, ground, as desired
- 1 tbsp. of oil, olive
- Optional: 2 tbsp. of lemon juice, freshly squeezed

For sauce

- 1/2 cup of tahini, sesame
- 1/4 – 1/2 cup of hot water, filtered
- 2 finely chopped garlic cloves
- 2 tbsp. of oil, olive
- 2 tbsp. of lemon juice, fresh
- 1 tbsp. of finely chopped parsley, fresh
- A pinch of cayenne
- Salt, kosher, as desired
- Pepper, ground, as desired

Instructions:

1. Preheat the oven to 400F.

2. Oil a cookie sheet. Scatter the sliced onions over it. Lay the fish on the onions with an inch between the fillets. Sprinkle with the seasonings and herb. Use the oil and lemon juice to drizzle.

3. Bake the fish in the 400F oven for 8-10 minutes till it's easily flaked using a fork.

4. Whisk 1/4 cup of the heated water and the tahini together.

5. Add the oil, lemon juice and garlic. Whisk well. Add the warmed water till the sauce has reached the consistency you desire. Add the parsley & seasonings as desired.

6. After the fish has cooked, top with the sauce. Serve promptly.

Kuwaiti Dessert Recipes…

Arabic Honey Cake

This cake is delicious and unique in many areas. It tastes so rich, as the syrup has caramelized on the sides and bottom.

Makes: 8 Servings

Cooking + Prep Time: 45 minutes

Ingredients:

- 3 eggs, large
- 1/2 cup of sugar, granulated
- 1/2 tsp. of vanilla extract, pure
- 1/3 cup of melted butter, unsalted
- 1/2 tsp. of baking powder, pure
- 1/2 cup + 1 tbsp. of flour, all-purpose

For the topping

- 1/2 cup of butter, unsalted
- 1/2 cup of sugar, granulated
- 1/3 cup of honey, organic
- 1/2 cup of almond slivers
- 1/2 tsp. of cinnamon, ground

Instructions:

1. Preheat the oven to 375F. Use non-stick spray to "grease" a round, 10-inch baking pan.

2. Beat the eggs, vanilla and sugar together till the mixture has whitened. Add the butter and combine well.

3. Sift the baking powder into the flour. Add it to the egg mixture, then gently mix. Pour in the prepared pan. Bake in the 375F oven for 10-12 minutes.

4. To prepare the topping, melt 1/2 cup of the butter in a pan on med. heat. Add the remainder of topping ingredients. Stir constantly while bringing to a boil.

5. When the first 10-12 minutes of the oven time ends, remove the cake. Pour the topping mixture gently over the cake.

6. Return the cake to the 375F oven for 15-20 minutes more till baked completely. Serve.

Khabees Al Nikhi

This is a fairly quick recipe to prepare unless you're making it for a large group of people. Rolling the baked balls in sesame seeds gives them a pleasing nutty taste.

Makes: Various # of Servings

Cooking + Prep Time: 1/2 hour

Ingredients:

- 1 cup of besan (chickpea flour)
- 3 to 4 tsp. of sugar, granulated + extra as desired
- Water, filtered – sufficient to cover sugar
- 2 tsp. of melted butter, unsalted
- A pinch of cardamom powder
- 1 tsp. of rose water, if available
- 5 or 6 dates, chopped
- Sesame seeds to garnish as desired

Instructions:

1. Preheat the oven to 350F.

2. To prepare the syrup, add the water and sugar to a non-stick pan and bring to a boil. Add the cardamom, butter & rose water.

3. To prepare the flour, roast the chickpea flour in a non-stick pan. It needs to be roasted, not raw.

4. Add the sugar water to the dough. Combine well. Fold in the dates. Make the dough into small-sized balls. Roll them in sesame seeds.

5. Bake the balls in 350F oven for 5-7 minutes. Serve.

Vanilla Custard – Kuwait Elbah

The saffron and cardamom give this treat its uniquely Arab taste. Although it is a dessert that is cooked for preparation, it should be served cold, so note the 4 hour refrigeration time.

Makes: 8 Servings

Cooking + Prep Time: 1 hour + 4 hours refrigeration time

Ingredients:

- 2 & 1/2 cups of milk, whole
- 5 eggs, large
- 1/2 cup of sugar, granulated + extra as desired
- A pinch of saffron
- 1/2 tsp. of cardamom
- 2 tsp. of vanilla, pure

Instructions:

1. Preheat the oven to 300F.

2. In a large-sized bowl, mix the vanilla, eggs and sugar together with a mixer. Add the milk. Continue to mix. Add the cardamom and saffron.

3. Ladle or pour the mixture in ramekins (oven safe material). Don't overfill them.

4. Place the ramekins in a roasting pan. Fill the pan 1/2-way with warmed water. Cover the entire pan with foil. Place the tray in the oven and cook at 300F for 40-45 minutes.

5. Remove when you can handle the pan safely. Allow to cool, then place the ramekins in the refrigerator for 4 hours to chill. Serve with tea or coffee.

Kuwaiti Sponge Cake

This classic cake is easy to prepare and is much like the sponge cakes made by many grandmothers. The flavors of saffron and cardamom make the perfect match for taste.

Makes: 6 Servings

Cooking + Prep Time: 45 minutes

Ingredients:

- 4 eggs, large
- 1/2 cup of sugar, granulated
- 1 tsp. of vanilla, pure
- 1 cup of flour, all-purpose
- 1 & 1/2 tsp. of powdered cardamom
- 1/2 tsp. of strands of saffron
- 2 tbsp. of seeds, sesame

Instructions:

1. Preheat the oven to 350F. Grease a 6" pan or tube pan. Sprinkle with 1/2 of the sesame seeds and set the pan aside.

2. Beat the eggs at a high setting by a mixer for about 5 minutes till they are foamy.

3. Add the sugar. Continue beating for a few minutes more. Add the vanilla. Beat for 1 minute more.

4. In a medium bowl, whisk the cardamom into the flour. Add to the egg mixture. Fold till combined well, with no lumps. Add the saffron threads. Mix once more.

5. Pour in the pan prepared in step 1. Pat the batter, ensuring that it is even. Sprinkle top with the remainder of sesame seeds.

6. Bake in the 350F oven for 25-30 minutes, until done.

7. Flip the cake onto a plate. You can serve warm or allow to cool and serve then.

Conclusion

This Kuwaiti cookbook has shown you…

How to use different ingredients to affect unique Middle Eastern tastes in many dishes.

How can you include recipes from Kuwait in your home repertoire?

You can…

- Make breakfast meals of shakshuka or menemen, which you may not have heard of before. They are just as tasty as they can be.
- Cook the soups and stews, which are widely served in Kuwaiti homes. Find ingredients in meat & produce or frozen food sections of your local grocery stores.
- Enjoy making tasty seafood dishes of Kuwait, including grouper and white fish. Fish is a mainstay in the Middle Eastern recipes, and there are SO many ways to make it great.
- Make dishes using vegetables and spices with Kuwaiti recipes. There is something about them that makes: the dishes more comforting.
- Make all kinds of the desserts like vanilla custard and honey cake, which anyone with a sweet tooth will love.

Share the recipes with friends and family!

About the Author

Allie Allen developed her passion for the culinary arts at the tender age of five when she would help her mother cook for their large family of 8. Even back then, her family knew this would be more than a hobby for the young Allie and when she graduated from high school, she applied to cooking school in London. It had always been a dream of the young chef to study with some of Europe's best and she made it happen by attending the Chef Academy of London.

After graduation, Allie decided to bring her skills back to North America and open up her own restaurant. After 10 successful years as head chef and owner, she decided to sell her business and pursue other career avenues. This monumental decision led Allie to her true calling, teaching. She also started to write e-books for her students to study at home for practice. She is now the proud author of several e-books and gives private and semi-private cooking lessons to a range of students at all levels of experience.

Stay tuned for more from this dynamic chef and teacher when she releases more informative e-books on cooking and baking in the near future. Her work is infused with stores and anecdotes you will love!

Author's Afterthoughts

I can't tell you how grateful I am that you decided to read my book. My most heartfelt thanks that you took time out of your life to choose my work and I hope you find benefit within these pages.

There are so many books available today that offer similar content so that makes it even more humbling that you decided to buying mine.

Tell me what you thought! I am eager to hear your opinion and ideas on what you read as are others who are looking for a good book to buy. Leave a review on Amazon.com so others can benefit from your wisdom!

With much thanks,

Allie Allen

Printed in Great Britain
by Amazon